# Contents

One of the lucky ones . . . . . . . 4

Taking off . . . . . . . . . . . . . . 6

The flight . . . . . . . . . . . . . . 8

Landing on the rig . . . . . . . . 10

A round trip . . . . . . . . . . . . . 12

Training . . . . . . . . . . . . . . . 14

Exciting past . . . . . . . . . . . . 16

Rough seas . . . . . . . . . . . . . 18

Emergency airlift . . . . . . . . . . 20

Another problem! . . . . . . . . . 22

Ferrying the bosses . . . . . . . . 24

What next? . . . . . . . . . . . . . 26

Writing a diary . . . . . . . . . . . 28

Glossary . . . . . . . . . . . . . . 30

Find out more . . . . . . . . . . . 31

Index . . . . . . . . . . . . . . . . 32

# One of the lucky ones

I am a helicopter pilot. I work for a company that flies workers to **oil rigs** out at sea. I'm lucky to have this job, because there aren't many jobs for helicopter pilots.

oil rig

# Diary of a Pilot

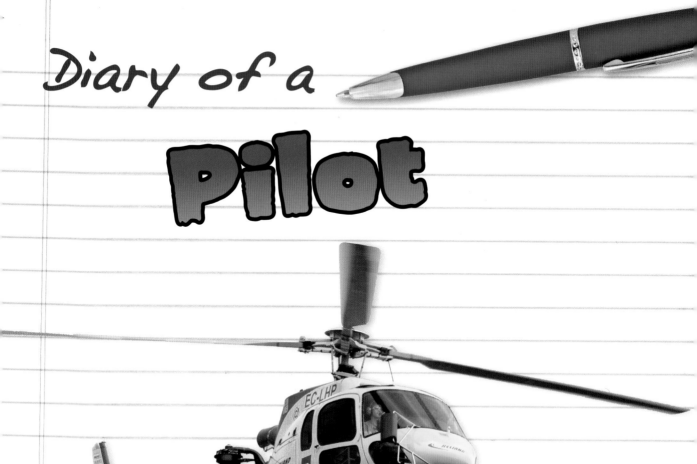

Angela Royston

Raintree is an imprint of Capstone Global Library Limited, a company incorporated in England and Wales having its registered office at 7 Pilgrim Street, London, EC4V 6LB – Registered company number: 6695582

www.raintreepublishers.co.uk
myorders@raintreepublishers.co.uk

Text © Capstone Global Library Limited 2014
First published in hardback in 2014
The moral rights of the proprietor have been asserted.

Edited by Daniel Nunn, Rebecca Rissman, and Catherine Veitch
Designed by Cynthia Della-Rovere
Picture research by Ruth Blair
Production by Victoria Fitzgerald
Originated by Capstone Global Library Ltd
Printed and bound in China by South China Printing Company Ltd

ISBN 978 1 406 26068 7 (hardback)
17 16 15 14 13
10 9 8 7 6 5 4 3 2 1

ISBN 978 1 406 26075 5 (paperback)
18 17 16 15 14
10 9 8 7 6 5 4 3 2 1

**British Library Cataloguing in Publication Data**
Royston, Angela.
Diary of a pilot.
629.1'3252-dc23
A full catalogue record for this book is available from the British Library.

**Acknowledgements**
We would like to thank the following for permission to reproduce photographs: Corbis pp. 4 (© Construction Photography), 11 (© Charles E. Rotkin), 14 (© Saed Hindash/Star Ledger), 21 (© doc-stock), 27 (© John Nakata); Getty Images pp. 6, 7 (Chris Ratcliffe/Bloomberg), 8 (Bernhard Limberger), 10, 22 (Alberto Incrocci), 12 (Julian Love), 17 (German Garcia/AFP), 19 (Arnulf Husmo), 20 (Jeff J Mitchell), 23 (Tyler J. Clements/U.S. Navy); Shutterstock pp. title page (© Natursports), contents page (© Leo Francini), 5 (© Ivan Cholakov), 15 (© James A. Harris), 18 (© Zastol`skiy Victor Leonidovich), 24 (© bikeriderlondon), 25 (© bajars), 28 diary (© Pavel Vakhrushev), 28 pen (© Phant); Superstock pp. 9, 26 (imagebroker.net), 13 (Justin Guariglia / age fotostock), 16 (Transtock).

Background and design features reproduced with permission of Shutterstock. Cover photograph of helicopter pilot reproduced with permission of Corbis (© Chris Crisman).

We would like to thank Olivia Milles for her invaluable help in the preparation of this book.

Every effort has been made to contact copyright holders of material reproduced in this book. Any omissions will be rectified in subsequent printings if notice is given to the publisher.

All the Internet addresses (URLs) given in this book were valid at the time of going to press. However, due to the dynamic nature of the Internet, some addresses may have changed, or sites may have changed or ceased to exist since publication. While the author and publisher regret any inconvenience this may cause readers, no responsibility for any such changes can be accepted by either the author or the publisher.

Some words are shown in bold, **like this**. You can find out what they mean by looking in the Glossary.

It is important to do safety checks while the helicopter is still on the ground.

Flying a helicopter takes skill. These aircraft have just one main engine. If the engine failed, I would have to make an emergency landing on the water!

This is my diary for one week.

# Taking off

## Sunday 12 May

This morning I flew to an **oil rig**. Before I set off I checked that the helicopter was filled with fuel and was ready for take off. Then I started the engine and the **rotors** turned above me.

rotors

engine

My passengers were workers employed on the oil rig, so they knew the journey well. When the **air traffic controller** gave us the **all clear**, we lifted off.

# The flight

The oil company insists that we leave and arrive on time. I flew at a safe height above the sea. There was a bit of wind, but not too much.

I kept a close eye on the flight instruments in the **cockpit** and reached the **oil rig** an hour later. I've flown there many times so I knew exactly where to land.

# Landing on the rig

When we reached the **oil rig**, another helicopter was just about to take off. I waited and then landed. The oil workers climbed out and got ready to start work.

Half an hour on an oil rig is enough for me, but the men work here for a week or longer. My return passengers were workers who were starting a week's break. They were keen to get going!

# A round trip

### Monday 13 May

Today I had Mick, a new pilot, with me. I showed him the three **oil rigs** we were flying to on the map. He typed the route into the **navigation system**.

navigation system

Mick was an experienced pilot, but flying to oil rigs was new to him. I showed him the best approach for landing on each rig. Then he flew the helicopter back to **base**.

13

# Training

Mick told me about his training. He went to flying school and got a licence to fly **fixed wing planes**. Then he trained to fly helicopters. It all cost him a lot of money.

fixed wing plane

I did it differently. I joined the army and they paid for my training. I flew helicopters that carried supplies from one **base** to another. On one flight, I had a heavy truck dangling below the helicopter!

# Exciting past

## Tuesday 14 May

Mick asked me what other jobs I'd done, so I told him about the years I spent flying police helicopters. It was fun – finding and tracking **suspects** from the air!

I also told him how I spent one summer fighting **wildfires**. It was exciting, but dangerous. We flew low over the sea and scooped up water to dump on the flames.

# Rough seas

## Wednesday 15 May

We had our own excitement today. There was a strong wind – too strong for our normal flights – but we had a call from one of the **oil rigs** that someone had hurt himself.

I took a doctor with us, but he didn't look too happy when we reached the rig. The wind was blowing so hard, I wasn't sure I could land safely.

# Emergency airlift

I hovered over the landing pad and the doctor was lowered down by **winch**. Luckily the wind then dropped for a few minutes, so I could land the helicopter on the rig.

winch

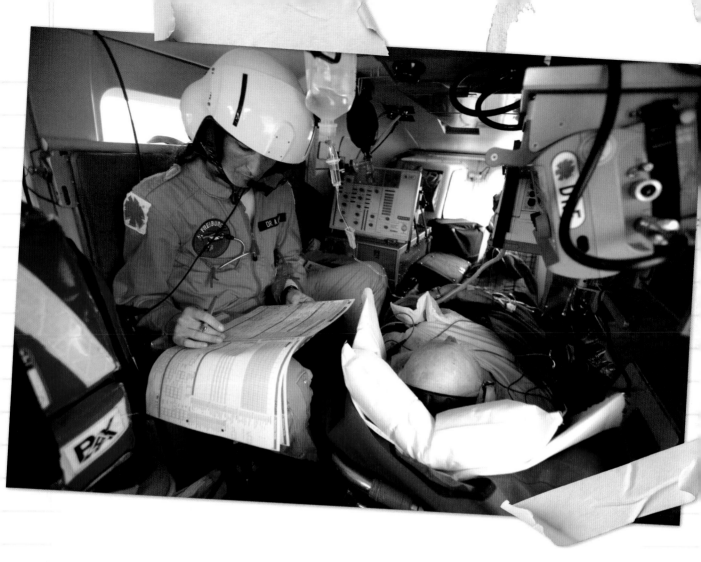

The worker's leg was badly broken. The doctor patched him up and then we lifted him into the helicopter. I set off and flew the injured man straight to the landing site at the hospital.

# Another problem!

## Thursday 16 May

I was more than halfway towards an **oil rig** today, when the **tail rotors** started playing up. I made it to the rig, but I couldn't solve the problem. I phoned head office.

They said there was a helicopter mechanic on the rig who could fix it. That was lucky! He managed to fix the problem. I hope nothing else goes wrong!

# Ferrying the bosses

## Friday 17 May

Today I flew three of the company directors from head office to one of the **oil rigs**. They asked me to wait until their meeting was over.

Then I flew them from the rig to one of the
company offices in another city. We landed
on the roof, then stayed overnight in a hotel.
The food in the restaurant was great!

# What next?

## Saturday 18 May

Next day I flew back to head office alone.
I thought about what job I'd like to do next.
The company has an **air rescue** branch, so
maybe I could do that?

Helicopters can rescue people from places that are very hard to get to.

Cameramen can get great shots from a helicopter.

I would also like to work for a television company, flying to disaster areas and big events. But everyone wants that job, and those who have it never leave!

# Writing a diary

A pilot writes a log of everything that happens. The log records facts such as the time the helicopter took off, what the weather was like, and the time it landed. This book, however, is a diary. It tells what happened from the pilot's point of view.

You can write a diary too! Your diary can describe your life – what you saw, what you felt, and the events that happened.

Here are some tips for writing a diary:

- Start each entry with the day and the date. You don't have to include an entry for every day.

- The entries should be in **chronological** order, which means that they follow the order in which events happened.

- Use the past tense when you are writing about something that has already happened.

- Remember that a diary is the writer's story, so use "I" and "my".

# Glossary

**air rescue** when a helicopter crew rescues people who are in danger at sea

**air traffic controller** person at an airport who tells pilots when they can take off and land

**all clear** message or signal that tells a pilot that it is safe to take off or land

**base** headquarters

**chronological** in order of time

**cockpit** place in the front of an aircraft where the pilot sits to fly the helicopter or aeroplane

**fixed wing planes** aeroplanes with wings that do not move

**navigation system** method of finding the way

**oil rig** metal structure that supports a huge drill. The drill digs through the rocks to reach oil that lies deep below the ground. Some oil rigs are out in the middle of the sea.

**rotors** blades that spin in a circle above a helicopter to lift it off the ground

**suspects** people who the police think may have committed a crime

**tail rotors** smaller blades at the back of the helicopter which stop the main rotors from making the helicopter spin

**wildfire** large fire that spreads quickly and destroys large areas

**winch** machine for winding in a thick wire or rope. On a helicopter, a winch is used to lift someone on or off the helicopter while it is in the air.

# Find out more

## Books

*Helicopters* (Machines on the Move), Andrew Langley
(Franklin Watts, 2011)

*Helicopters* (Rescue Vehicles), Valerie Bodden
(Creative Paperbacks, 2011)

*Helicopters* (Ultimate Machines), Rob Colson (Wayland, 2012)

## Websites

**encyclopedia.kids.net.au/page/he/Helicopter**
This website tells you in great detail about how a helicopter
works, and how it was invented.

**www.kidsinflight.org/hanger.html**
This website has interesting facts and games about flying,
the history of flight, pilots, and more.

**www.museumofflight.org/aircraft**
You don't have to visit Seattle in the USA to enjoy the
Museum of Flight. This website has photos and information
about several different types of aircraft.

**www.sciencemuseum.org.uk/visitmuseum/galleries/
flight.aspx**
The Science Museum in London includes several historic
aircraft in its Flight Gallery. You can also see them here on
their website.

# Index

air rescue 26, 30
air traffic controllers 7, 30
all clear 7, 30
army helicopters 15

cameramen 27
cockpits 9, 30

diary, keeping a 28–29

emergency airlifts 18–21
engines 5, 6

fixed wing planes 14, 30
flying schools 14

landing pads 20
log 28

mechanics 23

navigation systems 12, 30

oil rigs 4, 6, 9–11, 12, 13, 18–21, 24, 30

police helicopters 16

rotors 6, 22, 30

safety checks 5

tail rotors 22, 30
television companies 27
training 14–15

wildfires 17
winches 20, 30
winds 18, 19